Floral Elegance

18 Beautiful Cross Stitch and Needlepoint Designs

Susan Bates

Floral Elegance

18 Beautiful Cross Stitch and Needlepoint Designs

Susan Bates

Tuva Publishing
www.tuvayayincilik.com

Address: Merkez Mah. Cavusbasi Cad. No:71
Cekmekoy / Istanbul 34782 - TURKEY

Tel: +9 0216 642 62 62

Floral Elegance

First Print: 2011 / December, Istanbul
Second Print: 2015 / January, Istanbul

All Global Copyrights Belongs To
Tuva Tekstil San. ve Dış Tic. Ltd. Şti.

Language: English

Content: Cross Stitch

Editor in Chief: Ayhan DEMİRPEHLİVAN
Project Editor: Kader DEMİRPEHLİVAN
Designer: Susan BATES
Technical Advisor: K. Leyla ARAS
Graphic Design: Ömer ALP, Abdullah BAYRAKÇI
Asistant: Büşra ESER

ISBN: 978-605-5647-27-8

Printing House
Bilnet Matbaacılık - Biltur Yayın ve Hizmet A.Ş. Dudullu
Organize Sanayi Bölgesi 1. Cadde No:16 - Ümraniye
Istanbul / TURKEY

f facebook.com/TuvaYayincilik

t twitter.com/TuvaYayincilik

p pinterest.com/TuvaPublishing

Introduction

Many things inspire me to design embroidery designs, such as the flowers in my garden, textile designs and patterns, botanical prints, interior design magazines and books on many subjects, such as painting, design and gardening. In fact, many things that I see around me can inspire me!

As a child I loved to draw. I also helped my mother with her sewing. She taught me to sew and knit. I think it is this upbringing which has given me my love of sewing and other crafts. In later life I studied painting at college, and my love of textiles and pattern even found its way into my work, some of my paintings featured floral patterns!

After I left college I began to design my own needlepoint designs, in my spare time. I later sold these designs to publishing companies in the UK. In fact, I still sell my designs to publishing companies; my designs regularly appear in cross-stitch magazines in the UK.

For this book I really enjoyed designing the needlepoint designs, as well as the cross-stitch patterns, as it was really enjoyable for me to go back to the technique that first inspired me to start designing embroideries.

The designs in this book are mainly inspired by flowers; even the teacups and teapots are decorated with flowers. Flowers lend themselves really well to embroidery because of their organic shape and they have a timeless appeal. Although there is a rich tradition of flowers appearing in embroidery I have tried to give my designs a clean and contemporary look, using fresh colours and subtle shading.

In this book have designed patterns for a variety of projects, so that there are small pincushion designs, scissor cases and small pictures as well as the larger cushion and tablecloth designs. There are cross-stitch and needlepoint designs, so why not try a new technique if you have not done one of these techniques before.

Hopefully you will be inspired to make these designs and will enjoy stitching them as much as I have enjoyed designing them!

Susan Bates

Project Gallery

Tea and Biscuits

This design celebrates that great pastime of tea drinking! The delicate bone china
cup and saucer is decorated with little flowers and the soft rose patterned
wallpaper in the background gives the design a vintage feel. The soft colour
palette suggests calmness and relaxation!

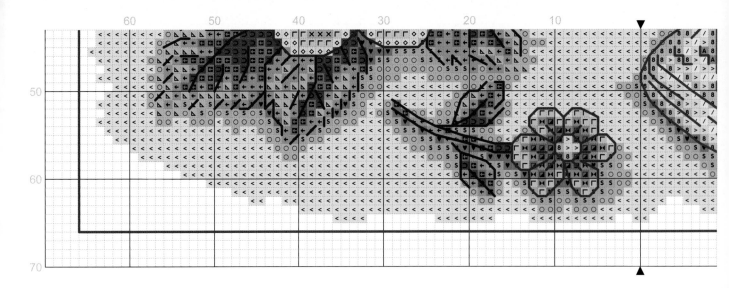

Mouliné
Stranded Cotton Art. 117

Cross Stitch			Half Cross Stitch	Backstitch
318	3761	962	727	413
Ecru	553	819	962	815
666	3828	703	164	351
3341	727	772	3823	319
3350	676	519	963	904
963	415	747		164
904	Blanc	554		3834
164	351	725		483
3760	967	3823		

Fabric: DMC 16 ct Aida Fabric (DM844/712)
Thread: DMC Stranded Cotton
Colour: Cream
Fabric Size: 50 x 50 cm
Design Size: 19 x 18 cm
Needle: DMC Tapestry Needle No:24
Cross Stitch: 2 strands
Backstitch: 1 strand
Stitch Count: 128 x 129

If you like, you can stitch edges of cup and saucer, centre of the flowers with the metallic thread.

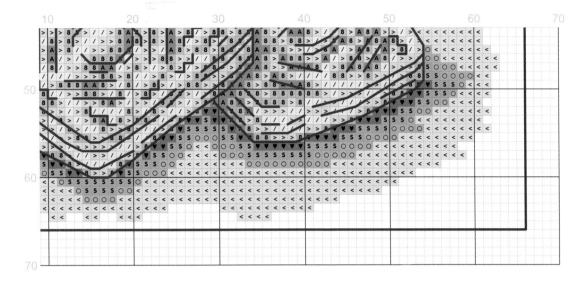

Cupcakes

The charm of a cupcake is that each one is decorated individually. These cupcakes are decorated with cream, cherries, redcurrants, icing and edible decorations. The pink, mauve and turquoise blue colour scheme adds a playfulness to the designs.

Cross Stitch

⊔⊔ 3810	∕∕ 712	ᴀᴀ 728		
−− 747	ꓯꓯ 434	ꓯꓯ 898		
ᴇᴇ 3804	ᴃᴃ 738	>> 3864		
\\ 151	3766	∶∶ Blanc		
ꜱꜱ 553	3801	436		
ᴏᴏ 727	ᴏᴏ 3806			
ᴏᴏ 3862	554			

Backstitch

/ 3842
/ 815
/ 3834
/ 909
/ 898
/ 3862

French Knot

● 815

DMC
Mouliné
Stranded Cotton Art. 117

Tablecloth

Fabric: DMC 16 ct Aida Fabric (DM844/712)
Thread: DMC Stranded Cotton
Colour: Cream
Fabric Size: 40 x 110 cm
Design Size: 48 x 48 cm
Needle: DMC Tapestry Needle No:24
Cross Stitch: 2 strands
Backstitch: 1 strand
French Knot: 2 strands
Stitch Count: 54 x 252
Final Size: 90 x 90 cm

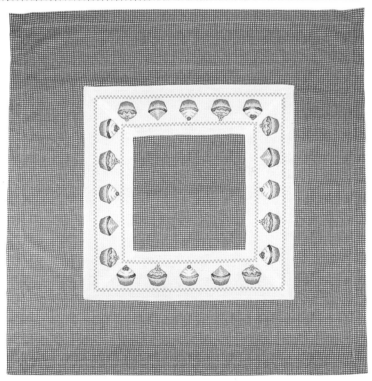

Book Cover

Fabric: DMC 16 ct Evenweave Fabric (DM844/712)
Thread: DMC Stranded Cotton
Colour: Cream
Fabric Size: 14 x 14 cm
Design Size: 7 x 8 cm
Needle: DMC Tapestry Needle No:24
Cross Stitch: 2 strands
Backstitch: 1 strand
French Knot: 2 strands
Final Size: 24 x 17 cm
Stitch Count: 48 x 54

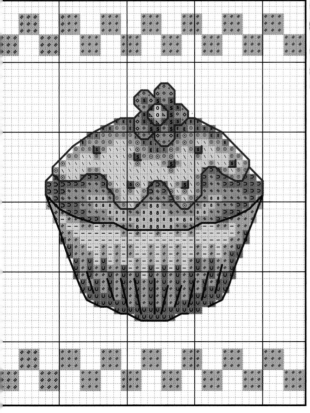

DMC
Mouliné
Stranded Cotton Art. 117

Cross Stitch						Backstitch	
3810		712		728		3842	
747		434		898		815	
3804		738		3864		3834	
151		3766		Blanc		909	
553		3801		436		898	
727		3806				3862	
3862		554					

23

Coaster

Fabric: DMC 16 ct Aida Fabric
(DM844/712)
Thread: DMC Stranded Cotton
Colour: Cream
Fabric Size: 13 x 14 cm
Design Size: 8 x 8 cm
Needle: DMC Tapestry Needle No:24
Cross Stitch: 2 strands
Backstitch: 1 strand
French Knot: 2 strands
Final Size: 9 x 9 cm
Stitch Count: 51 x 54

Mouliné
Stranded Cotton Art. 117

Cross Stitch			Backstitch	
3810	712	728	3842	
747	434	898	815	
3804	738	3864	3834	
151	3766	Blanc	909	
553	3801	436	898	
727	3806		3862	
3862	554			

French Knot

● 815

Greeting Card

Fabric: DMC 16 ct Aida Fabric
(DM844/712)
Thread: DMC Stranded Cotton
Colour: Cream
Fabric Size: 13 x 14 cm
Design Size: 8 x 8 cm
Needle: DMC Tapestry Needle No:24
Cross Stitch: 2 strands
Backstitch: 1 strand
French Knot: 2 strands
Final Size: 9 x 9 cm
Stitch Count: 51 x 54

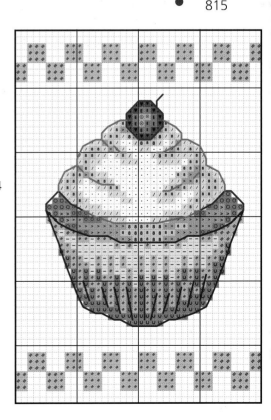

Tea in the Garden

What better way to enjoy the garden than to sit and relax with a cup of tea and some cake! The view from my bedroom window into my garden inspired this design. The chairs and table and some of the plants in the pots were drawn from my garden, but some of it is fantasy – it's how I would like my garden to look, all year around!

Cross Stitch

3831	3815	435	818	518	Blanc	
3326	3765	Ecru	209	828	3821	
3837	3766	3024	367	3826		
319	433	3078	472	676		
368	783	335	563	738		

Backstitch

/ 815 / 803

/ 550 / 3031

/ 319 / 433

/ 367

Mouliné
Stranded Cotton Art. 117

30

Cross Stitch

3831	3815	435	818	518	Blanc	
3326	3765	Ecru	209	828	3821	
3837	3766	3024	367	3826		
319	433	3078	472	676		
368	783	335	563	738		

Backstitch

/ 815   / 803
/ 550   / 3031
/ 319   / 433
/ 367

DMC
Mouliné
Stranded Cotton Art. 117

Fabric: DMC 16 ct Aida Fabric
(DM266/712)
Thread: DMC Stranded Cotton
Colour: Cream
Fabric Size: 55 x 50 cm
Design Size: 31 x 25 cm
Needle: DMC Tapestry Needle No:24
Cross Stitch: 2 strands
Backstitch: 1 strand
Stitch Count: 167 x 188

Floral Bouquets

Each floral bouquet features a variety of flowers, from nasturtiums and morning glories to daffodils, pansies and roses, to name a few! The designs work well by themselves but look beautiful when displayed as a trio.

Wild Flowers Bouquet

Mouliné
Stranded Cotton Art. 117

Cross Stitch		Backstitch	
	3328	/	815
	3824	/	319
	367	/	920
	3819	/	645
	898	/	820
	436		
	3853		
	726		
	648		
	Blanc		
	799		
	747		
	760		
	225		
	703		
	772		
	434		
	920		
	972		
	3078		
	712		
	798		
	3840		

Wild Flowers Bouquet

Fabric: DMC 14 ct Aida Fabric (DM844/712)
Thread: DMC Stranded Cotton
Colour: Cream
Fabric Size: 45 x 40 cm
Design Size: 21 x 15 cm
Needle: DMC Tapestry Needle No:24
Cross Stitch: 2 strands
Backstitch: 1 strand
Stitch Count: 107 x 81

Small Daffodils Bouquet

Mouliné
Stranded Cotton Art. 117

Cross Stitch		Backstitch	
■	550	/	550
= = / = =	341	/	434
↑ ↑ / ↑ ↑	976	/	699
s s / s s	973	/	831
: :	746		
8 8 / 8 8	911		
o o / o o	369		
> > / > >	745		
⋈ ⋈ / ⋈ ⋈	831		
▲ ▲ / ▲ ▲	3746		
◇ ◇ / ◇ ◇	3747		
⊙ ⊙ / ⊙ ⊙	742		
\ \ / \ \	727		
■	699		
/ / / / /	954		
- - / - -	3865		
T T / T T	834		

Small Daffodils Bouquet

Fabric: DMC 14 ct Aida Fabric (DM844/712)
Thread: DMC Stranded Cotton
Colour: Cream
Fabric Size: 45 x 40 cm
Design Size: 18 x 14 cm
Needle: DMC Tapestry Needle No:24
Cross Stitch: 2 strands
Backstitch: 1 strand
Stitch Count: 101 x 76

Small Roses Bouquet

Fabric: DMC 14 ct Aida Fabric
(DM844/712)
Thread: DMC Stranded Cotton
Colour: Cream
Fabric Size: 45 x 40 cm
Design Size: 19 x 15 cm
Needle: DMC Tapestry Needle No:24
Cross Stitch: 2 strands
Backstitch: 1 strand
Stitch Count: 105 x 80

Small Roses Bouquet

DMC
Mouliné
Stranded Cotton Art. 117

Cross Stitch

	3804		223	
	151		309	
	3721		761	
	224		948	
	3833		744	
	316		912	
	3865		772	
	505	**Backstitch**		
	966	/	815	
	3806	/	814	
	819	/	3740	
		/	319	

41

Summer Flowers in a Vase

This design reminds me of heady summer days when all the flowers in the garden are in bloom. It's lovely to bring some flowers into the home and admire them. The advantage of this floral display is that the flowers in this vase never fade!

Fabric: DMC 14 ct Aida Fabric
(DM244/712)
Thread: DMC Stranded Cotton
Colour: Cream
Fabric Size: 65 x 55 cm
Design Size: 32 x 41 cm
Needle: DMC Tapestry Needle No:24
Cross Stitch: 2 strands
Backstitch: 1 strand
Stitch Count: 210 x 180

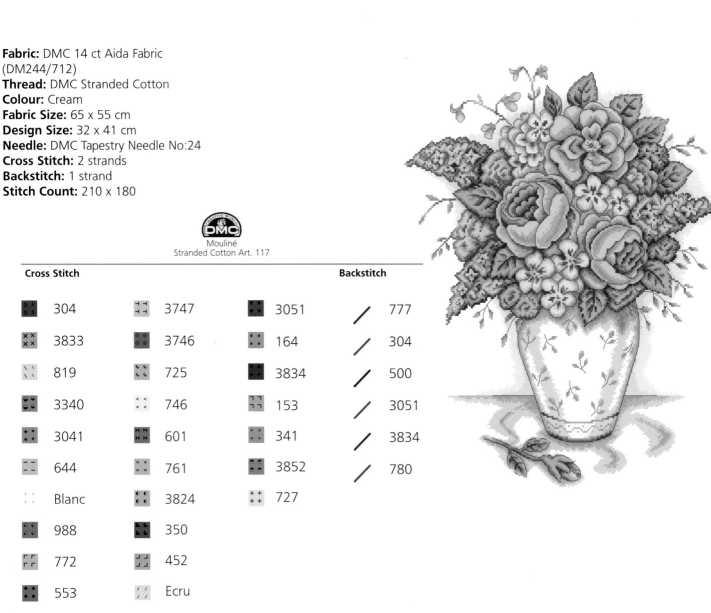

DMC
Mouliné
Stranded Cotton Art. 117

Cross Stitch			Backstitch
304	3747	3051	777
3833	3746	164	304
819	725	3834	500
3340	746	153	3051
3041	601	341	3834
644	761	3852	780
Blanc	3824	727	
988	350		
772	452		
553	Ecru		

My Garden

This design features lots of little gardening motifs; individual flowers
such as lavender, pansies and little seedlings, as well as insects that
we see in the garden. The garden bench in the centre reminds me
of lazy days in the garden when you can sit back and admire all the
hard work that you've done!

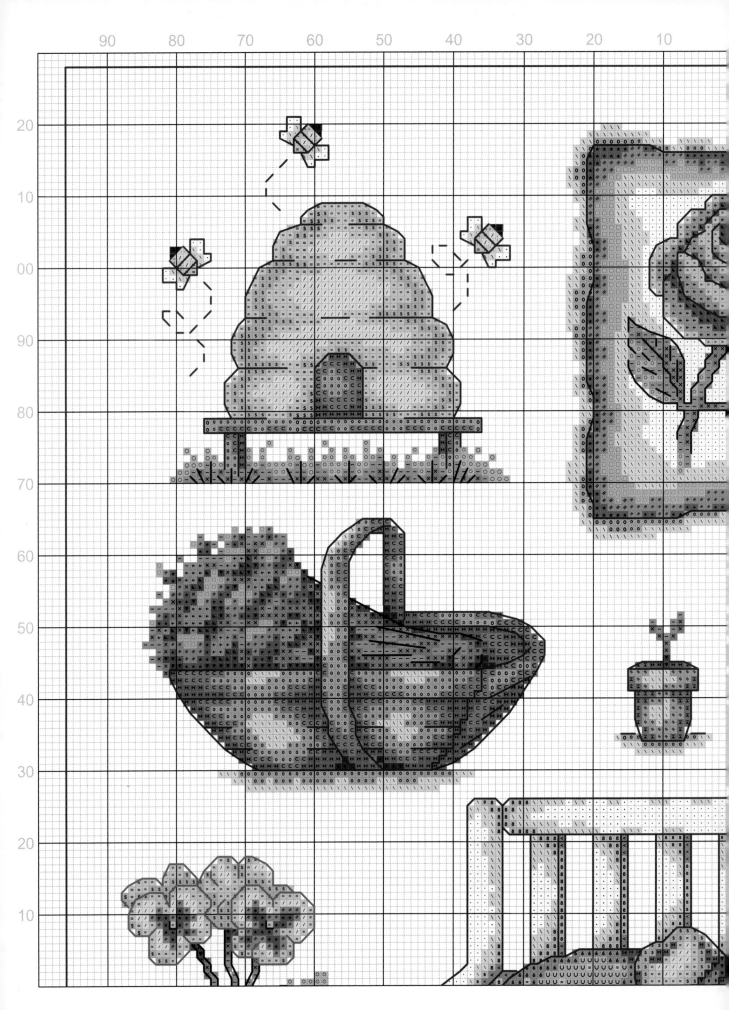

Fabric: DMC 14 ct Aida Fabric
(DM444/712)
Thread: DMC Stranded Cotton
Colour: Cream
Fabric Size: 65 x 55 cm
Design Size: 27 x 37,5 cm
Needle: DMC Tapestry Needle No:24
Cross Stitch: 2 strands
Backstitch: 1 strand
French Knot: 2 strands
Stitch Count: 243 x 178

DMC
Mouliné
Stranded Cotton Art. 117

Cross Stitch

▓	3799	▸	225
8	415	▪	351
∷	Blanc	▪	333
✦	3326	▫	211
▓	817	✕	703
U	353	○	772
◆	209	Z	913
▼	910	▪	3761
▬	3819	▫	725
◢	955	▓	938
▼	518	C	436
S	977	◆	3827
▨	3078		
▓	434		
○	738		
▓	3853		
◄	414		
＼	Ecru		
▓	335		

Backstitch

╱	3799
╱	815
╱	550
╱	500
╱	434
╱	938

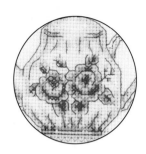

Red and White China Tablecloth

The red and white china teapot and teacups look lovely against the crisp white linen of the tablecloth. The red decoration on the china updates the design and gives the traditional motifs a more contemporary feel.

Mouliné
Stranded Cotton Art. 117

Cross Stitch		Backstitch	
■ 666	⌗ 3340	╱ 413	╱ 666
⊙⊙ 3824	▪▪ 169	╱ 169	╱ 3340
═ 415	╱╱ 3866	╱ 304	
∵ Blanc			

Fabric: Rico Design Ready to Stitch Table Cloth (Art. 17875.50.21)
Thread: DMC Stranded Cotton
Colour: White
Fabric Size: 90 x 90 cm
Design Size: 46 x 46 cm
Needle: DMC Tapestry Needle No:24
Cross Stitch: 2 strands
Backstitch: 413: 1 strand   **666:** 1 strand
           169: 1 strand   **3340:** 2 strands
           304: 1 strand

Final Size: 90 x 90 cm
Stitch Count: 203 x 47

Position of Motifs

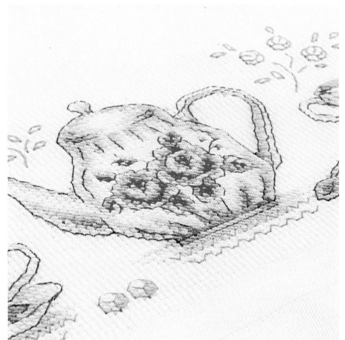

Five O'clock Tea

Soft pink roses adorn the teapot and teacups of this design and make me think of afternoon tea. You can use this design to make a lovely tea towel, repeat the design to decorate a tablecloth or frame it to make a pretty picture.

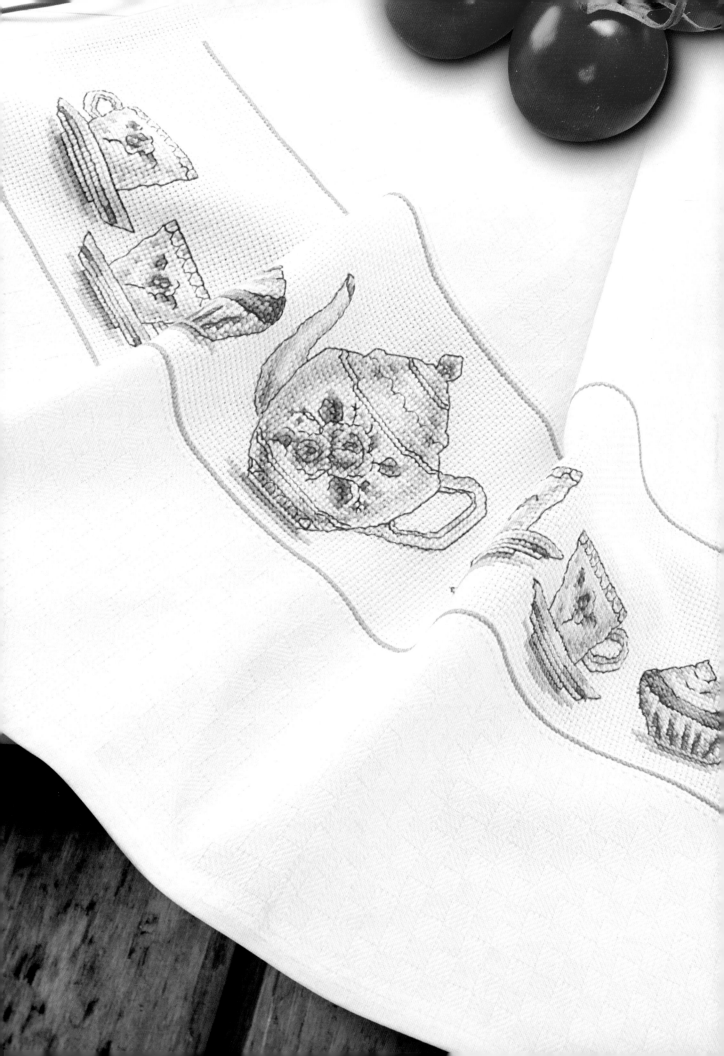

Mouliné
Stranded Cotton Art. 117

Cross Stitch				Backstitch	
✦✦	601	◦◦	962	╱	498
‹‹	151	▴▴	169	╱	601
══	415	╱╱	3866	╱	535
∶∶	Blanc	◆◆	937	╱	986
››	581	◦◦	472	╱	801
★★	434	▪▪	436		
++	738				

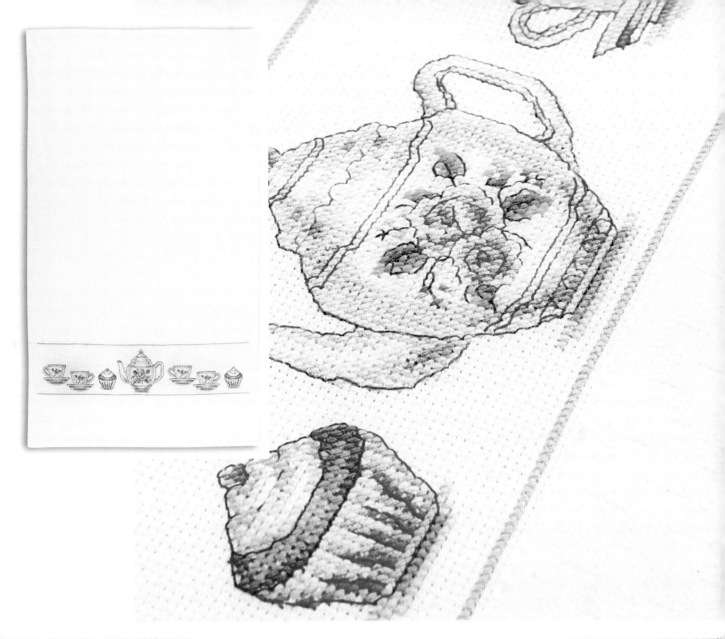

Fabric: DMC 14 ct Aida Fabric
(DM222/Blanc)
Thread: DMC Stranded Cotton
Colour: White
Fabric Size: 50 x 15 cm
Design Size: 45 x 10 cm
Needle: DMC Tapestry Needle No:24
Cross Stitch: 2 strands
Backstitch: 1 strand
Final Size: 45 x 10 cm
Stitch Count: 252 x 56

Tapestries

Floral Footstool

The circular nature of this design is very pleasing to the eye and it lends itself very well to a design for a stool. The corals, fuchsia pinks and purples of the roses and other flowers make a stunning design and the black background adds to the drama!

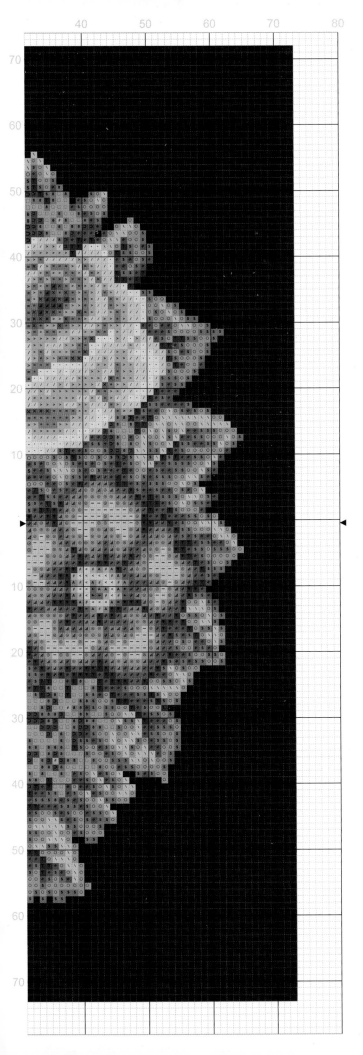

Fabric: DMC Penelope Antique Canvas
(DT 401)
Thread: DMC Colbert Tapestry Wool
Colour: Natural Linen
Fabric Size: 63 x 63 cm
Design Size: 31 x 31 cm
Needle: DMC Tapestry Needle No:18
Final Size: 43 x 43 cm
Stitch Count: 144 x 144
Only half cross stitch

**Fill the background according
to the size of your footstool.**

Colbert Tapestry Wool
Art. 486

Half Cross Stitch

▼▼	7157	↘↘	7153
◢◢	7605	⊙⊙	7133
– –	7171	← ←	7487
A A	7485	# #	7725
< <	7078	◢◢	7207
✗ ✗	7758	= =	7759
> >	7004	∕ ∕	7003
··	Ecru	▉	7385
◆◆	7749	s s	7548
⊙⊙	7549	∖∖	7420
⊃⊃	7014	8 8	7523
□□	7251	■	Noir

Scissor Case
&Pincushion

If you're new to tapestry why not try making these small designs
first? The rose motifs are easy to stitch and the small scale means
that you will finish them quickly!

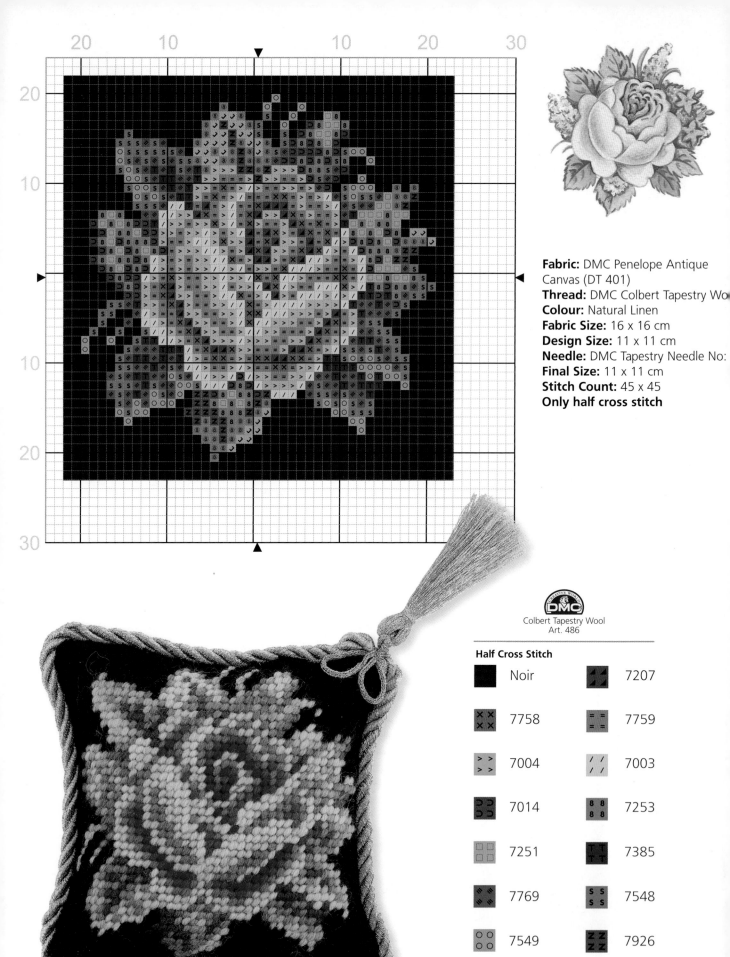

Fabric: DMC Penelope Antique
Canvas (DT 401)
Thread: DMC Colbert Tapestry Wo[ol]
Colour: Natural Linen
Fabric Size: 16 x 16 cm
Design Size: 11 x 11 cm
Needle: DMC Tapestry Needle No:
Final Size: 11 x 11 cm
Stitch Count: 45 x 45
Only half cross stitch

DMC
Colbert Tapestry Wool
Art. 486

Half Cross Stitch

■	Noir	◥◣	7207
××	7758	==	7759
>>	7004	//	7003
⊐⊐	7014	8 8	7253
□□	7251	TT	7385
◈◈	7769	SS	7548
○○	7549	ZZ	7926
8 8	7927	✓✓	7828

76

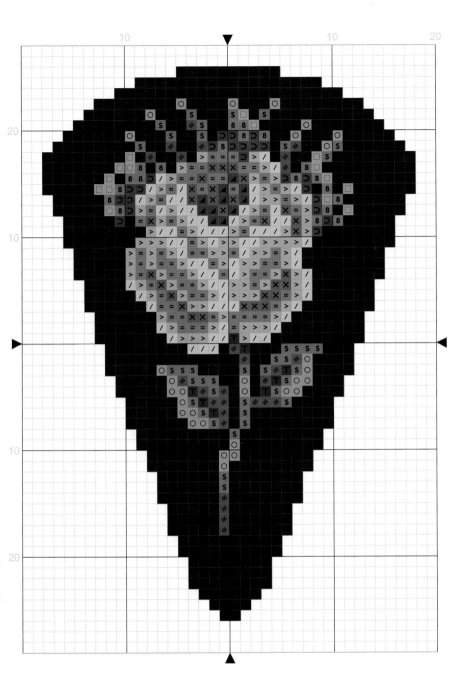

Colbert Tapestry Wool
Art. 486

Half Cross Stitch

■	Noir	T T	7358
▨	7769	S S S	7548
O O O O	7549	◤◥	7207
X X X X	7758	= = = =	7759
> > > >	7004	/ / / /	7003
⊃⊃ ⊃⊃	7014	8 8 8 8	7253
▢▢ ▢▢	7251		

Fabric: DMC Penelope Antique Canvas (DT 401)
Thread: DMC Colbert Tapestry Wool
Colour: Natural Linen
Fabric Size: 16 x 20 cm
Design Size: 13 x 9 cm
Needle: DMC Tapestry Needle No:18
Final Size: 9 x 13 cm
Stitch Count: 36 x 55
Only half cross stitch

Pink Rose Cushion

For this design I was inspired by botanical prints. The rich shades of pink in the petals and the blues and greens of the border and leaves are offset beautifully by the soft cream background. The little rose in each corner add charm to the overall design.

Fabric: DMC Penelope Antique Canvas (DT 401)
Thread: DMC Colbert Tapestry Wool
Colour: Natural Linena
Fabric Size: 50 x 50 cm
Design Size: 40 x 40 cm
Needle: DMC Tapestry Needle No:18
Final Size: 40 x 40 cm
Stitch Count: 159 x 159
Only half cross stitch

DMC
Colbert Tapestry Wool
Art. 486

Half Cross Stitch

8 8 / 8 8	7650
. . / . .	Ecru
↑ ↑ / ↑ ↑	7107
s s / s s	7004
\ \ / \ \	7191
+ + / + +	7056
■	7408
C C / C C	7042
◇ ◇ / ◇ ◇	7040
/ / / / /	7599
z z / z z	7110
⊙ ⊙ / ⊙ ⊙	7005
▽ ▽ / ▽ ▽	7003
♥ ♥ / ♥ ♥	7444
> > / > >	7055
■	7326
# # / # #	7041

81

Large Roses Tapestry Cushion

The large blooms on this cushion give it a contemporary feel and the rich palette of pinks, mauves and purples are contrasted against the two different shades of green leaves and the subtle cream background shade.

Fabric: DMC Penelope Antique Canvas (DT 401)
Thread: DMC Colbert Tapestry Wool
Colour: Natural Linen
Fabric Size: 50 x 50 cm
Design Size: 41 x 41 cm
Needle: DMC Tapestry Needle No:18
Final Size: 41 x 41 cm
Stitch Count: 158 x 158
Only half cross stitch

DMC
Colbert Tapestry Wool
Art. 486

Half Cross Stitch

< < < <	7500
C C C C	7257
= = = =	7253
. . . .	7191
S S S S	7153
⊙ ⊙ ⊙ ⊙	7804
✦ ✦ ✦ ✦	7327
> > > >	7322
A A A A	7386
⋰ ⋰	7549
▫ ▫	7425
◢ ◢ ◢ ◢	7353
■	7372
╱ ╱	7210
◇ ◇ ◇ ◇	7251
╱ ╱ ╱ ╱	7151
◤ ◣	7157
■	7999
6 6 6 6	7927
■	7540
▫ ▫ ▫ ▫	7770
○ ○ ○ ○	7420
➜ ➜ ➜ ➜	7367
╲ ╲	7470

Rose and Paisley Tapestry Cushion

This cushion was inspired by Victorian designs which often used the rose motif alongside the paisley pattern. The curling shape of the roses in the centre and the organic shape of the paisley motifs contrast well with the linear background. The black and cream background also adds an interesting dynamic to the design.

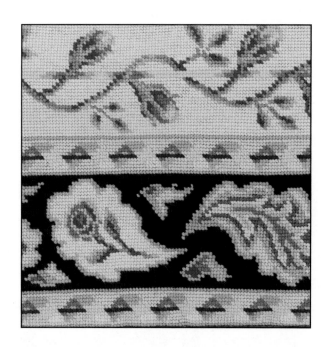

Fabric: DMC Penelope Antique
Canvas (DT 401)
Thread: DMC Colbert Tapestry
Wool
Colour: Natural Linen
Fabric Size: 50 x 50 cm
Design Size: 41 x 41 cm
Needle: DMC Tapestry Needle
No:18
Final Size: 41 x 41 cm
Stitch Count: 158 x 158
Only half cross stitch

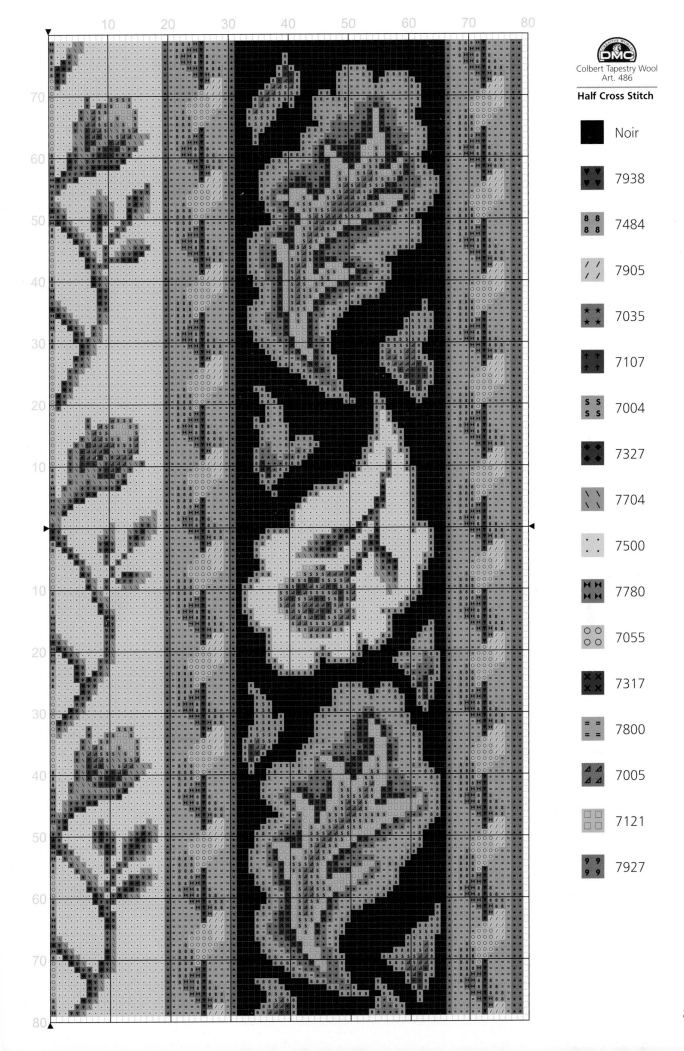

DMC
Colbert Tapestry Wool
Art. 486

Half Cross Stitch

■	Noir
♥	7938
8 8	7484
/ /	7905
★ ★	7035
↑ ↑	7107
S S	7004
◆ ◆	7327
\ \	7704
· ·	7500
►◄ ►◄	7780
○ ○	7055
✕ ✕	7317
= =	7800
◢ ◢	7005
☐ ☐	7121
9 9	7927

Three Roses Tapestry Cushion

The three roses in the centre of this design make a bold statement on the black background and the paisley borders to the left and right add decorative detail to the background.

Fabric: DMC Penelope Antique
Canvas (DT 401)
Thread: DMC Colbert Tapestry Wool
Colour: Natural Linen
Fabric Size: 60 x 45 cm

Design Size: 38 x 28 cm
Needle: DMC Tapestry Needle No:18
Final Size: 38 x 28 cm
Stitch Count: 158 x 118
Only half cross stitch

DMC
Colbert Tapestry Wool
Art. 486

Half Cross Stitch

■	Noir
	7758
	7121
	7447
	7851
	7999
	7326
	7040
	7045
	7108
	7004
	7244
	7520
	7110
	7761
	Ecru
	7850
	7853
	7329
	7323
	7548
	7389
	7005
	7026
	7056
	7500

93

The Stitches

This section shows how to work the stitches used in the book. When following these instructions, note that stitching is over one block of Aida or two threads of evenweave.

Starting and Finishing Thread

To start off your first length of thread, make a knot at one end and push the needle through to the back of the fabric, about 3cm (1^{1}/4in) from your starting point, leaving the knot on the right side. Stitch towards the knot, securing the thread at the back of the fabric as you go. When the thread is secure, cut off the knot.

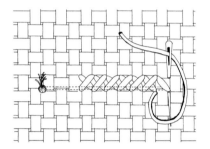

To finish off a thread or start new threads, simply weave the thread into the back of several stitches.

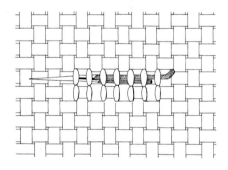

Backstitch

Backstitch is indicated on the charts by a solid coloured line. It is worked around areas of completed cross stitches to add definition, or on top of stitches to add detail.

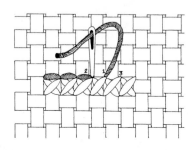

To work backstitch, pull the needle through the hole in the fabric at 1 and back through at 2. For the next stitch, pull the needle through at 3, then push to the back at 1, and repeat the process to make the next stitch. If working backstitch on an evenweave fabric, wovrk each backstitch over two threads.

Bullion Knots

These knots are wonderful for adding three-dimensional texture to designs.

Follow the following figure, right, bringing the needle up at 1 and down at 2, but do not pull thread through (a). Stab the needle up at 1 again but bring it only halfway through the material (b). Holding needle from below, wind the thread around it until the number of twists equals the distance between 1 and 2 (c). Holding the top of the needle and thread firmly with thumb and finger, draw the needle through, loosening the coil of threads with your hand as you do so, to allow the needle to pass through freely (d).

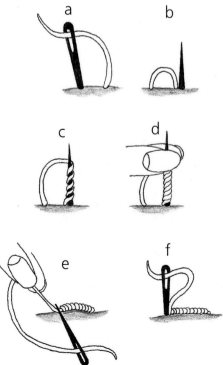

Place the needle against the end of the twist, at the same time pulling the thread until the knot lies flat on the material.
If any bumps appear in the knot, flatten these by stroking them beneath the twist with the needle, at the same time pulling the thread (e). Put needle into the fabric, close to the end of the twist, and pull through firmly (f).

Cross Stitch

Each coloured square on a chart represents one complete cross stitch. Cross stitch is worked in two easy stages. Start by working one diagonal stitch over one block of Aida or two threads of evenweave, then work a second diagonal stitch over the first stitch, but in the opposite direction to form a cross.

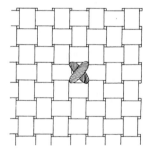

A cross stitch on Aida fabric.

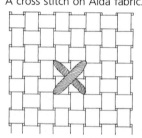

A cross stitch on evenweave fabric.

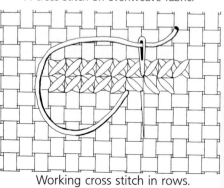

Working cross stitch in rows.

Cross stitches can be worked in rows if you have a large area to cover. Work a row of half cross stitches in one direction and then back in the opposite direction with the diagonal stitches to complete each cross. The upper stitches of all the crosses should lie in the same direction to produce a neat effect.

Quarter Cross Stitch

If you chose to work a design on a double mesh canvas using wool (yarn), a quarter cross stitch should be used instead of a three-quarter cross stitch. To work, start at one corner of the canvas mesh and work in the same direction as any half stitches but insert the needle at the corner of the square.

Half Cross Stitch

This stitch is also used if you chose to work a design on canvas in tapestry wool (yarn), replacing whole cross stitches with half stitches. A half cross stitch is simply one half of a cross stitch, with the diagonal facing the same way as the upper stitches of each complete cross stitch.

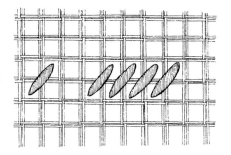

Three-quarter Cross Stitch

A small coloured triangle taking up half a chart square represents a three-quarter cross stitch. Forming fractional stitches is less accurate on Aida than on evenweave because the centre of the Aida block needs to be pierced.

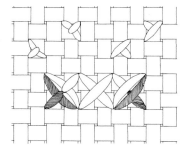

Work the first half of a cross stitch in the normal way, then work the second diagonal stitch in the opposite corner but insert the needle at the centre of the cross, forming three-quarters of the complete stitch. A square showing two smaller coloured triangles in opposite corners indicates that two three-quarter cross stitches will have to be worked back to back, sharing holes.

French Knots

These are small knots used for details, indicated on charts by coloured dots.

To work a French knot, bring the needle through to the front of the fabric, just above the point you want the stitch placed. Wind the thread once around the needle and, holding the twisted thread firmly, insert the needle a little away from its starting position. Two tips for working French knots: never rush them and never go back into the same point where your thread came up or your knot will pull through to the back.

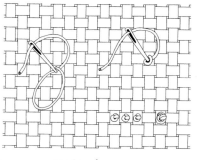

Long Stitch

These are used to work some flower stems and are indicated on charts by a straight coloured line – refer to the instructions for the colour. Work long stitches on top of cross stitches. To work long stitch, pull the needle through the fabric at the point indicated on the chart and push it through at the other end shown on the chart, to make a long, straight stitch on top of the fabric. Repeat for the next stitch, carrying the thread across the back of the fabric to the next starting point.

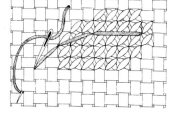

Susan Bates

I currently live in Brighton, on the south coast of England. I have been an embroidery designer for some time now. I went to college to study fine art and have a degree in painting. However sewing is something I that I have always loved. As a child my mother taught me to sew and knit and it is this that has inspired me to learn all about sewing, and eventually embroidery.

After I went to college I worked in a shop in London that sold hand-painted needlepoint kits. The lady who owned and ran the store had a great eye for colour and design. Working there inspired me to start designing my own needlepoint designs. (I think the shop is still open to this day, although I worked there quite a long time ago!)

Alongside doing my own needlepoint designs, (at home as a hobby initially), I also worked for a couple of large department stores in London that sold designer hand knitting yarns and patterns. We were encouraged to knit up the designs in the store to inspire the customers to buy the patterns and yarn and knit the designs themselves. I eventually left these jobs to pursue my design work.

Initially I sold some of my needlepoint designs to a publishing company in London and they then asked me to start designing cross-stitch designs. After this I was asked to start designing cross-stitch designs for other publishing companies in England. I now currently do most of my design work for Origin Publishing Ltd in Bristol.

I have done a few other things as well, such as training to be an art teacher and teaching knitting and sewing classes to adults.